Waiting Here For You

Waiting Here For You

An Advent Journey of Hope

Louie Giglio

with Dudley Delffs

 HarperChristian Resources  passionpublishing

The day God visits you has come,

 the day your watchmen sound the alarm.

 Now is the time of your confusion. . . .

But as for me, I watch in hope for the LORD,

 I wait for God my Savior;

 my God will hear me.

MICAH 7:4,7

Waiting Here for You Bible Study Guide
© 2023 by Louie Giglio

Requests for information should be addressed to:
HarperChristian Resources, 3900 Sparks Dr. SE, Grand Rapids, Michigan 49546

ISBN 978-0-310-16934-5 (softcover)
ISBN 978-0-310-16935-2 (ebook)

HarperChristian Resources titles may be purchased in bulk for church, business, fundraising, or ministry use. For information, please e-mail ResourceSpecialist@ChurchSource.com.

First Printing August 2023 / Printed in the United States of America

23 24 25 26 27 LBC 5 4 3 2 1

Contents

SESSION 4: GOD IS WAITING FOR YOU

Welcome

Christmas. It's right around the corner. You may be looking forward to it and the opportunities it brings to get together with family and friends. Or you might be dreading it and all the stress it creates. In either case, it's easy to get caught up in the hustle surrounding the season and forget the reason why we celebrate Christmas in the first place. This is the goal of this study—to help you focus more intentionally on what Jesus' birth in Bethlehem means for you today.

Christmas is much more than just a memorable day of gathering with family and friends to open presents and eat a delicious meal. It's more than shopping, wrapping, cooking, eating, and watching your favorite holiday movies. The season of Advent in historical church traditions—the four weeks leading up to December 25th—reminds us that the story of Christmas is one of *waiting*.

The people of Israel waited 400 years for the promised Messiah to arrive. For those four centuries, there was no prophet, no voice, no promise, and no act of God recorded in Scripture. When Malachi penned the final words of his book in the Old Testament, nothing followed . . . just silence. Generation after generation, the people of Israel kept their faith alive by holding on to the promise that someday the Lord would send the promised Deliverer to them.

Finally, "when the fullness of the time had come" (Galatians 4:4 NKJV), the voices of angels broke that silence, announcing to a group of bewildered shepherds, "Today in the town of David a Savior has been born to you; he is the Messiah, the Lord. This will be a sign to you: You will find a baby wrapped in cloths and lying in a manger" (Luke 2:11–12).

At Christmastime, we celebrate the birth of Jesus—God's beloved Son—born to this world in human form. We sing songs like "Joy to the World" to commemorate the incarnational origin story of our Savior. But the hope of Christmas is also about waiting and about the hope we find in the midst of our waiting. Because while we're waiting, God is still working.

Even though we may feel stuck and wonder when, how, or even if our wait will end, God is actively moving forward with His master plan for our lives. We may think nothing is happening when we're weary and at the end of our rope. We are afraid to believe that our wait could ever be over. But then something suddenly shifts. There is the moment when God reveals Himself and His plan and His power in our lives, just as He did in a manger in Bethlehem.

Advent invites you to slow down, to view this Christmas season through a whole new lens, and to discover a faithful God in the midst of your waiting. It prompts you to think about your own seasons of silence and realize those times are never wasted when you are waiting on God. But even more, Advent helps you recognize that God is always with you in the waiting.

Louie Giglio

How to Use This Guide

If you picked up this guide, you are likely wanting something more in this Christmas season. Perhaps you struggle with stress, anxiety, depression, grief, or loneliness this time of year. As the shadows of winter fall, you may think about all that you've lost—loved ones, relationships, opportunities. Or perhaps you usually enjoy Christmas, but you're going through something—an illness, an injury, a financial struggle, a battle with addiction, a concern about your marriage, or a fear about what your children are facing.

Or maybe you feel drawn to this study for other reasons. Things seem to be going well and you are grateful for so many blessings . . . yet there's a longing to experience Christmas in a deeper way. Even as you enjoy the holiday season, you're mindful of those who suffer around you, those in need, and family and friends who are struggling. Wherever you find yourself, this study will help you discover the real meaning of Advent—as a season of waiting in which you can recognize all God is doing in your life as you wait on Him and with Him.

Before you begin, keep in mind there are a few ways you can go through this material. You can experience this study with others in a group (such as a Bible study, Sunday school class, or any other small-group gathering), or you may choose to go through the content on your own. Either way, know that the videos for each session are available for you to view at any time by following the instructions provided on the inside cover of this study guide.

Overview

Each session in this study is divided into two parts: (1) an overview section designed for both individual and group engagement, and (2) a personal study section that you can do on your own throughout the week. The overview section provides a basic framework for that week's focus and offers ways to get the most out of the video content and to engage the key ideas that were presented in the teaching. Each session includes the following:

- **Welcome:** A short opening note about the topic of the session to introduce the big idea and to get you started.
- **Connect:** A couple questions to get you thinking about the topic and to break the ice if you are part of a group study.
- **Watch:** An outline of the key points covered in each video teaching along with space for you to take notes as you watch each session.
- **Discuss:** Questions to help you (and your group) reflect on the teaching material presented and apply it to your lives.
- **Respond:** A short personal exercise to help reinforce the key ideas.
- **Pray:** A place for you to record prayer requests and praises for the week.

If you are doing this study in a group, make sure you have your own copy of the study guide so you can write down your thoughts, responses, and reflections—and so you have access to the videos via streaming. You will also want to have a copy of *Waiting Here for You*, as reading it alongside this study will provide you with deeper insights.

If you are part of a group study, please keep these points in mind:

- **Facilitation:** You will want to appoint someone to serve as a facilitator of your group. This person will be responsible for starting the video and keeping track of time during discussions and activities. If *you* have been chosen for this role, there are some resources in the back of this guide that can help you lead your group through the study.

- **Faithfulness:** Your group is a place where tremendous growth can happen as you reflect on the Bible, ask questions, and learn what God is doing in other people's lives. For this reason, be fully committed and attend each session so you can build trust and rapport with the other members.

- **Friendship:** The goal of any small group is to serve as a place where people can share, learn about God, and build friendships. Seek to make your group a safe place. Be honest about your thoughts and feelings, but also listen carefully to everyone else's thoughts, feelings, and opinions. Keep anything personal that your group members share in confidence so that you can create a community where people can heal, be challenged, and grow spiritually.

If you are going through this study on your own, make the experience part of your Advent celebration of the Christmas season. Consider connecting with one or two other friends or family members who are also completing this study or observing Advent. Touch base with them at least once each week and compare your experiences and observations.

Personal Study

The personal study is for you to work through on your own during the week. Each exercise is designed to help you explore the key ideas in the video teaching and delve into passages of Scripture that will help you apply those principles to your life. Go at your own pace, doing a little each day—or tackle the material all at once. Remember to spend a few moments in silence to listen to whatever God might be saying to you.

Note that if you are doing this study as part of a group and you are unable to finish (or even start) these personal studies for the week, you should still attend the group time. Be assured that you are still wanted and welcome even if you don't have your "homework" done. This personal study is intended to help you hear what God is saying and apply His words to your life. So . . . as you go through it, listen for Him to speak to you, and ready your heart and mind to experience His presence while you wait.

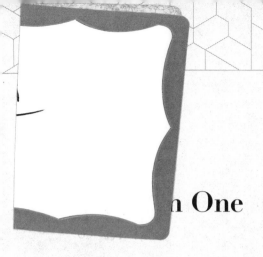

God Is Working While You Wait

*The LORD is good to those whose hope is in him,
to the one who seeks him; it is good to wait quietly
for the salvation of the LORD.*

LAMENTATIONS 3:25–26

Welcome | READ ON YOUR OWN

From an early age, we grasp the idea of waiting . . . and we rarely like it. We are told by our parents (and others) that we have to wait our turn, wait until after dinner to get dessert, wait until Christmas morning to open all those wonderfully wrapped presents we see under the tree. As we grow older, we get more accustomed to waiting . . . but oftentimes we don't like it any better. We wait to finish school and receive a degree. We wait to get the job we've always dreamed of. We wait for that "right" person to finally come into our lives.

We wait . . . and then wait some more.

You're likely waiting on something right now. Maybe you're anticipating an upcoming trip that you've been planning for months or expecting a baby to arrive. You might be anxiously awaiting results from the doctor for yourself or someone you love. You could be waiting to see if an important relationship will survive challenges you both are facing. As you wait, you may be facing circumstances that stir up feelings of impatience, fear, uncertainty, and anxiety.

The people of Israel understood what it meant to wait . . . and we can assume they didn't like it either. God had promised through His prophets to send them a Messiah. But year after year, generation after generation, century after century, God's promise did not come to pass. Yet, as we will discover in this session, this didn't mean that God was doing nothing while they waited. When Jesus finally arrived, the Bible makes it clear that God had been working each and every moment to reveal His perfect plan at just the right time.

The same is true in your life. Regardless of what you are waiting on, or how long you've been waiting, you can trust that God is working as you wait.

Connect | 15 MINUTES

If you or any of your group members don't know each other, take a few minutes to introduce yourselves. Then discuss each of these questions:

- How does your family typically celebrate Christmas?

- Why did you decide to do this study? What do you hope to experience?

Watch | 20 MINUTES

Now it's time to dive into the video for this session, which you can access by playing the DVD or through streaming (see the instructions provided). Note any key concepts that stand out to you.

OUTLINE

I. The advent season is about remembering that God will come through for us.
  A. The story of the Messiah's arrival on earth is a story of waiting.
  B. God had promised His people, the Israelites, that He would send a redeemer.
  C. Throughout the Old Testament we find prophecies foretelling the Messiah, including Genesis 3:15, Deuteronomy 18:15–19, Psalm 110, and Isaiah 52:13–53:12.
II. Four hundred years had passed between the writing of the last verse of the Old Testament and the arrival of Jesus.
  A. There was no prophet, voice, promise, or recorded act of God during this time.
  B. But then, into the silence, angels appeared to shepherds and told of the birth of the Messiah.
  C. What this says is that even in the silence—in the waiting—God is still working.
III. All of us know what it means to be stuck in a time of waiting . . . and we rarely like it.
  A. You are likely in some place of waiting—waiting for a child to come home, a spouse to tell the truth, a test result, a pregnancy, a court sentence, a miracle to happen.
  B. You may be waiting for the holiday season to end so normal life can resume.
  C. We are not good at waiting, but the reality is that God is not often in a hurry.
IV. While we are in this time of waiting, we need to keep our focus on God's promises.
  A. We are waiting on many things, but what we're really waiting for is Jesus to come.
  B. When He returns to this world, He will put an end to the pain of this planet.
  C. Advent is knowing that Jesus has already won and not losing sight of that truth.
V. In Revelation 21, we get a picture (and promise) of how it will all come down in the end.
  A. We are getting a new heaven and a new earth (verses 1–2), where we experience God's very presence (verse 3), comfort, and joy (verse 4).
  B. Everything that is currently wrong with this world we will be set right in that day.
  C. This is where our season of waiting ends—the future that God has in store for us.

NOTES

Discuss | 35 MINUTES

Discuss what you just watched by answering the following questions.

1. We all know how Christmas is celebrated in our society, but how familiar are you with the tradition of Advent? What role has it played in your past Christmas seasons?

2. As discussed in the video, Advent is about waiting in expectation and remembering that God comes through on His promises. What are you waiting on right now? What does it mean for you to wait in expectation that God will come through on His promises?

3. The Lord promised that He would send a Messiah . . . and then His people waited in silence for 400 years for Jesus to arrive. Why do you think God made His people wait? How do you typically respond when you don't hear from God as quickly as you want?

4. Is there something significant that you continue to wait on God to provide? What evidence have you glimpsed, if any, that God is working while you wait?

5. How does the birth of Jesus give you hope that God is actively working for your good and on your behalf, even though you may not be able to fully see it?

Respond | 10 MINUTES

As you close out this session, take a few minutes on your own to consider what you are waiting on God to provide in your life. Use the space below to write out a prayer to Him. Use the prompts to get started, but make your prayer as personal as possible.

- What are some things you are currently waiting on God to provide?
- How long have you been waiting for them?
- Which one takes priority for you or seems most urgent right now? Why?
- How do you usually feel about waiting on God to provide these things for you?

Pray | 10 MINUTES

Praying for one another is one of the most important things you can do as a community. Make this time more than just a "closing prayer" to end your group experience by openly sharing your needs and how you're asking God to come through for you. (If you feel comfortable, you might even want to share the prayer that you wrote to God in the Respond section.) Use the space below to write any requests mentioned so you can pray for them in the week ahead.

Name   Request

Personal Study

As you go through this Advent study, a key part of your growth will involve studying Scripture. The Bible, which we call *God's Word*, contains life-giving words from your heavenly Father, exemplified by Jesus, and illuminated by His Holy Spirit. As you dive into these exercises, listen for God to speak to you and remain receptive to hearing His voice. For the fullest study experience, we encourage you to read the *Waiting Here for You* devotional alongside this study. Use the daily reading schedule on the following page to help guide you along.

Weekly Reading Plan

Before You Begin	Read "What Are You Waiting For?" and "The Story of Christmas Grace" (pages 7–15 in the *Waiting Here for You* devotional)
Day 1	Complete Study 1 and read "Just the Right Time" (page 18)
Day 2	Complete Study 2 and read "God Works While We Wait" (page 22)
Day 3	Complete Study 3 and read "Choose God's Way" (page 26)
Day 4	Go through the Connect & Discuss questions with a friend or someone in the group and read "Jesus Sets You Free" (page 30)
Day 5	Complete the Worship While You Wait exercises and read "By His Wounds You Are Healed" (page 34)
Before Next Week	Read "Seek and You Will Find" (page 38) and "Compassion Over Consumption" (page 42)

Study One

Waiting Room

Most people develop different ways of coping with having to wait. Think back to a time when you were at a doctor's office or in line for an event where you were forced to wait longer than anticipated. You may have observed that some people fidget and complain, clearly upset at having to wait but trying to contain their frustration. A few may act entitled or appear outraged by having to wait along with everyone else, demanding attention and special treatment. Others may seem stoic and quiet, withdrawing into themselves as they try to ignore or deny the situation. Most people seek to distract themselves by texting, checking email, surfing social media, or listening to a podcast or music on their phone. A couple might exchange small talk with one another, offering opinions on the weather, sports, or why they are there.

Regardless of how you tend to respond when forced to wait, the reality is that it rarely speeds up the process.

When waiting on larger goals, dreams, and outcomes, it can be challenging to know how to be present in the midst of waiting. Most of us grow impatient. We want to know what to expect and when to expect it. We want things to happen on *our* time. While we know we cannot speed up the process of waiting or hurry God along, we still don't know what to do with ourselves during the in-between time while we wait. Which is why learning to experience God even while we wait makes all the difference.

1. How would you describe your usual response to unexpected delays that result in waiting longer than you want? When was the last time you experienced this?

> How long, LORD? Will you forget me forever?
>   How long will you hide your face from me?
> How long must I wrestle with my thoughts
>   and day after day have sorrow in my heart?
>   How long will my enemy triumph over me?
>
> PSALM 13:1–2

2. This psalm includes references to waiting on God and expresses the writer's frustration over not feeling heard or seen by God in the midst of his distress. The psalmist's sentiments remind us that our frustration is a normal, human response to the urgency we feel in our need. When have you felt like God had forgotten you or was hiding His face from you? How did you respond to this sense of waiting on God to speak or reveal Himself to you?

3. What's the longest you have ever waited on something you desperately wanted? How would you describe your relationship with God during that season of waiting?

4. How do you usually spend the weeks leading up to Christmas? Why is waiting for Christmas to arrive different from many of the other things you wait on in life?

Part of the fun of the Christmas season, especially for children, is the anticipation of the day itself. Waiting on Christmas to arrive, though, usually doesn't feel like that long of a time, given the full calendars and hectic pace. And we may even take comfort in knowing that regardless of what we do or leave undone, Christmas still comes. We can know with certainty that the hours, days, and weeks will pass leading up to Christmas Day.

5. Other than Christmas, when was the last time you waited on something with a fixed period of waiting? Perhaps you custom ordered something that took weeks or months to make and deliver, or you might have been counting down the semesters until graduation. Does waiting on something with a fixed endpoint seem easier to you than waiting on something without a clear timeline of fulfillment? Why?

Father, I am here waiting for You.
My heart and hands are open to Your
purposes and plans for my life.
Give me the patience I so desperately
need and lead me in my waiting.
Though my feelings may not be there
just yet, I believe You are moving on my
behalf right this minute, protecting,
defending, preparing, providing.
Give me grace to keep trusting in You
in the face of the gale force winds of
doubt that are blowing all around me.
Anchor my heart in You. Amen.

Study Two

What Are You Waiting For?

From the moment we first became conscious of time as children, we learned that waiting required anticipating something that would happen in the future. Sometimes, the length of our waiting could be measured—two hours until lunchtime, three days until the ballgame, four weeks until we could open presents at Christmas. But other times, it was less certain as to exactly when we would receive whatever we were waiting for.

As you saw in the teaching for this week, this is the kind of waiting—the one without a clear timeframe or calendar date—the Jewish people endured for generations. God had promised to send them a Messiah. He gave them clues about His identity through the prophets, but no one knew when this Messiah would arrive on the scene. As the centuries passed and the Israelites were invaded by one powerful empire after another, they must have often quoted the words of Psalm 13:1 to one another: "How long, LORD? Will you forget [us] forever?"

The people of Israel knew what God had promised them, but they didn't know the Lord's timing in delivering on His promise. Sometimes, the same is true in our lives. We know that we are in a season of waiting, but we don't know how or when God will act. Regardless, it's important for us to be clear on what we need from God and want Him to do in our lives—and then trust that He will provide in His own way and in His own timing. In this way, we stay engaged with God during the waiting and actively look for how He is providing for us. This prevents us from drifting away from God or passively resigning ourselves to whatever happens.

"But you, Bethlehem Ephrathah,
    though you are small among the clans of Judah,
out of you will come for me
    one who will be ruler over Israel,
whose origins are from of old,
    from ancient times."

MICAH 5:2

1. The Israelites only had clues from the prophets as to what the Messiah would do once He arrived on earth. Based on this passage in Micah, what might the people have assumed about the role of the Messiah and the actions He would immediately take?

2. Everyone is usually waiting on something in that uncertain, indefinite category—meeting your future spouse, moving for your dream job, starting a family. Most people are waiting on several things at once, which can compound the frustration. Naming the things you are waiting on can help you recognize the tension you are carrying while waiting. List as many items as possible below, briefly describing them, and note when you hope it happens, as well as when you think it will actually come to pass.

Waiting for . . .	When I hope it happens	When I think it will actually happen

"So I say to you: Ask and it will be given to you; seek and you will find; knock and the door will be opened to you. For everyone who asks receives; the one who seeks finds; and to the one who knocks, the door will be opened. Which of you fathers, if your son asks for a fish, will give him a snake instead? Or if he asks for an egg, will give him a scorpion? If you then, though you are evil, know how to give good gifts to your children, how much more will your Father in heaven give the Holy Spirit to those who ask him!"

LUKE 11:9–13

3. In order to avoid waiting, we may be reluctant to ask God for what we need and want. We may assume He already knows (which He does), so there's no need to ask. Yet Jesus tells us that seeking God and asking for what we desire is an important part of relating to God as our heavenly Father. If you haven't asked God for the items you listed above, what has prevented you from doing so? How does Jesus reveal the way God wants to respond to us when we ask Him for what we're seeking?

For God alone, O my soul, wait in silence,
    for my hope is from him.
He only is my rock and my salvation,
    my fortress; I shall not be shaken.
On God rests my salvation and my glory;
    my mighty rock, my refuge is God.

PSALM 62:5–7 ESV

4. The psalmist reminds us that waiting is inherently about waiting on God as our singular source of hope. When we are focused on Him, we find strength, refuge, and security amidst our uncertainty. What are some other things you have put your hope in while waiting on God? How well did they distract you from your impatience and frustration with waiting?

5. How aware are you of what you are waiting for? Take a moment to consider each of the following statements and respond with whether you agree or disagree.

I am very aware of what I am waiting on in my life right now.

| 1 | 2 | 3 | 4 | 5 | 6 | 7 | 8 | 9 | 10 |

Disagree Strongly   Agree Strongly

I frequently pray and ask God to grant me what I'm waiting on.

| 1 | 2 | 3 | 4 | 5 | 6 | 7 | 8 | 9 | 10 |

Disagree Strongly   Agree Strongly

I tell trusted others about what I'm waiting on and ask for their prayers.

| 1 | 2 | 3 | 4 | 5 | 6 | 7 | 8 | 9 | 10 |

Disagree Strongly   Agree Strongly

My faith in God will be impacted by whether I get what I'm waiting on or not.

| 1 | 2 | 3 | 4 | 5 | 6 | 7 | 8 | 9 | 10 |

Disagree Strongly   Agree Strongly

Promises in the Process

It's a scene we love to imagine. We read about it, sing about it in carols, and see it depicted in nativity scenes. There they are, some shepherds with their flocks out in the darkness, encamped on the rolling pastures outside Bethlehem. As the sun sets on another day, they build a fire, prepare something to eat, check on their sheep, and draw lots to see who will take the first watch while the others sleep. Then—BAM!—the night sky lights up brighter than day and angels appear, telling the shepherds not to be afraid, that they have good news—the best possible news—to share.

This scene is a study in contrasts, for sure. A normal night turns into a life-changing, history-making moment after which nothing will be the same. One minute these guys are counting sheep, and the next they're dazzled by angels. As sudden as this announcement seems, though, it didn't happen quickly.

A Savior had been promised throughout the Scriptures, beginning all the way back in Genesis 3:15 when God described how the Enemy would be overcome. Moses talked about a prophet that God would raise up at a later time (see Deuteronomy 18:15–19). David referred to the Messiah as both a king and a priest (see Psalm 110). The prophet Isaiah foretold how the Messiah would be a suffering servant (see Isaiah 52:13–53:12). Studying God's Word, it's clear He has a plan for saving His people. But after the prophet Malachi, no mention was made of the Messiah, or anyone else, for four centuries.

Suddenly, it all came together at once. God had not forgotten His promises nor abandoned His people. He was working actively throughout that long period of silence to bring His plan to fruition that night in Bethlehem. Generation after generation, people couldn't see what He was doing and didn't get the confirmation they wanted. But God's promises remained alive in the process of their waiting.

You may find yourself in a similar place today. You know what God has promised, but you feel stuck in the process of waiting. But just as God revealed to the shepherds that night, the Lord can move suddenly and unexpectedly to fulfill His promises.

1. Why do you suppose God's promises about sending the Messiah are sprinkled throughout the Scriptures prior to those four hundred years of silence? What does His silence for that lengthy period tell us about how God views time compared to our view?

2. What promises from God's Word speak directly to you and what you're waiting for? How often do you remind yourself of these promises?

"The LORD your God will raise up for you a prophet like me from among you, from your fellow Israelites. You must listen to him. For this is what you asked of the LORD your God at Horeb on the day of the assembly when you said, 'Let us not hear the voice of the LORD our God nor see this great fire anymore, or we will die.' The LORD said to me: 'What they say is good. I will raise up for them a prophet like you from among their fellow Israelites, and I will put my words in his mouth. He will tell them everything I command him.'"

DEUTERONOMY 18:15–18

3. Why do you suppose Moses emphasized that God would raise up a prophet similar to himself, someone who was also an Israelite? What's the significance of God's response to His people's request in the passage above?

> Surely he took up our pain
>   and bore our suffering,
> yet we considered him punished by God,
>   stricken by him, and afflicted.
> But he was pierced for our transgressions,
>   he was crushed for our iniquities;
> the punishment that brought us peace was on him,
>   and by his wounds we are healed.
> We all, like sheep, have gone astray,
>   each of us has turned to our own way;
> and the LORD has laid on him
>   the iniquity of us all.
>
> ISAIAH 53:4–6

4. What resonates or stands out to you in this prophetic description of the Messiah from Isaiah? What promises in this passage still apply to you today in the midst of your waiting?

And there were shepherds living out in the fields nearby, keeping watch over their flocks at night. An angel of the Lord appeared to them, and the glory of the Lord shone around them, and they were terrified. But the angel said to them, "Do not be afraid. I bring you good news that will cause great joy for all the people. Today in the town of David a Savior has been born to you; he is the Messiah, the Lord. This will be a sign to you: You will find a baby wrapped in cloths and lying in a manger."

Suddenly a great company of the heavenly host appeared with the angel, praising God and saying,

"Glory to God in the highest heaven,
  and on earth peace to those on whom his favor rests."

LUKE 2:8–14

5. How does the angel's message make it clear that God has kept His promises, even after 400 years? What hope do you find in this scene in the midst of what you're waiting for?

Connect & Discuss

Waiting can often be a lonely business. Usually, the more important the object of our waiting becomes, the more we may be tempted to carry the burden of waiting alone. Yet throughout God's Word, He makes it clear that waiting is a communal process—something shared so that we can remind one another of God's commitments to us, encourage one another when struggling, and celebrate together in the fulfillment of His promises.

Take some time today to connect with someone and share something you're waiting for right now. It doesn't have to be the most personal item on your list, but it should be more than just *for Christmas to arrive.* If you're part of a group completing this study, reach out to a fellow group member and discuss some of your insights from this first week's session. Use any of the following prompts to help begin your time of sharing and waiting together.

What Is one of your struggles this Christmas season? What would make your burden lighter?

Beyond Christmas, what are you waiting on that you would like to ask others to pray about?

What's one of God's promises that you're clinging to right now?

What's the hardest part of waiting, especially for things with no end in sight?

What is something you uncovered this week that changed how you are anticipating Christmas?

How can you pray for one another in the midst of waiting together this Advent season?

Worship While You Wait

Waiting in silence can feel unbearable, but God doesn't ask us to stifle our voices and suppress our feelings while we wait. He wants us to know that He cares, which means He wants to hear us give words to all that may be swirling around inside us. Of course, He already knows what we're thinking and feeling, but He wants us to experience the relational intimacy of sharing that with Him directly—in conversation and communication with Him.

Certain thoughts and emotions have likely risen up in you as you've begun this study. What you do with those thoughts and emotions will shape how you move through your times of waiting. Knowing you feel heard, seen, and accepted by your heavenly Father will provide you with confidence as you seek patience and peace during these in-between times. Prayer, worship, praise, and solitude will help you stay connected with God during this time.

For centuries, people have honored Advent by using a specially designated wreath that marks the passing of each week. Traditionally, the wreath was composed of evergreen branches. It included four candles in a circle and one "Christmas candle" in the center. There is nothing magical about using an Advent wreath, but it may enhance a sense of being intentional as you pause during this full season. Choosing to practice a personal Advent time alone with God often facilitates the peace, joy, and wonder we all long to experience at Christmas.

So as you go through this study, spend some time worshiping while you wait, using an Advent wreath of your choosing (or making) and lighting the corresponding number of candles. You will be provided with some questions or prompts each week, but the goal is simply to rest and listen to God as you reflect on the meaning of Christ's birth in your life. For this first week, choose a day and time that you can use consistently as your Advent moment with God. Purchase or make a simple wreath and find a spot where you can enjoy uninterrupted silence for at least fifteen minutes. Light one candle to signify this first week of Advent. Then use the prompts below to help you slow down and reflect as you draw closer to God.

> What responsibilities and burdens are weighing on you this week? As they come to mind, release them to God and surrender them to His sovereign ways.

How would you like God to meet you this Christmas season? What do you need most from Him to enjoy the intangible gifts during this time of year?

Reflect on this past week and your experience completing the personal studies. What stands out or resonates most with you? What does this tell you about what it means to wait on God?

Spend a few minutes quietly stilling your heart before God, listening to His Spirit. What do you sense that He is saying to you?

Come, Thou long expected Jesus

Born to set Thy people free;

From our fears and sins release us,

Let us find our rest in Thee

Israel's strength and consolation,

Hope of all the earth Thou art;

Dear desire of every nation,

Joy of every longing heart.

Born Thy people to deliver,

Born a child and yet a King,

Born to reign in us forever,

Now Thy gracious kingdom bring.

By Thine own eternal Spirit

Rule in all our hearts alone;

By Thine all sufficient merit,

Raise us to Thy glorious throne.

"COME, THOU LONG EXPECTED JESUS"
CHARLES WESLEY (1707–1788)

Session Two

God Will Use Your Waiting

But if we hope for what we do not yet have, we wait for it patiently.

ROMANS 8:25

Welcome | READ ON YOUR OWN

If you fly often enough, you will inevitably encounter dreaded delays. They may be weather-related due to a storm or high winds, the result of airline staffing issues, or a traffic bottleneck at the airport. Whatever the cause, waiting on your flight to take off can be especially stressful when you don't know the cause of the delay. Eventually, you discover that something essential was taking place during the interval—a mechanical problem was corrected, the pilot finally arrived, the runway and plane were cleared of ice.

The same is true when you're waiting on God. You may not understand why He seems to be taking longer than you thought or why unexpected obstacles have popped up. You keep waiting and praying and hoping, all the while wondering why it's taking so long. Maybe you even wonder if God has forgotten you or if you misinterpreted how He's guiding you.

Surely, the people of Israel experienced some of those same thoughts and feelings during those hundreds of years they spent waiting on the prophecies about the Messiah to be fulfilled. Each generation may have wondered if they would see the Promised One arrive and restore Israel. Each generation likely wrestled with a sense of disappointment as they realized they were apparently not going to live to see God's promise realized.

However, those faithful to God knew that the Lord had not forgotten them or rescinded His promise—even if they didn't experience it the way they wanted. They understood He was still at work in their lives and in the events of Israel, even if they couldn't see it with their eyes or comprehend it with their minds. God's ways are on a different schedule than the ones we tend to live by, but He continues working in and through us as we wait.

Connect | 15 MINUTES

Start your group session by discussing these questions together:

- How do you typically handle flight delays or postponed travel plans?

- What assumptions, if any, do you tend to make while waiting? Do you assume delays could be avoided with better planning—or that they're often necessary for things to fall into place?

Watch | 20 MINUTES

Now it's time to dive into the video for this session, which you can access by playing the DVD or through streaming (see the instructions provided). Note any key concepts that stand out to you.

OUTLINE

I. We can have hope for our future, knowing one day God will set all things right.
   A. Still, we must admit that things in this world right now are very wrong.
   B. We have to acknowledge that some of us are going through a difficult season this Christmas. This includes recognizing ways you are struggling right now.

II. God allows us to choose the object of our fixation in a world that is not right.
   A. While it's easy to fixate on the crises in life, we can make the conscious choice to fixate on Christ.
   B. In the storms of life, we learn to practice "spiritual replacement"—focusing on Jesus without ignoring the painful reality of this world.
   C. We remember Jesus was also in an advent season of waiting.

III. Luke's Gospel tells about a storm that occurred in the disciples' lives.
   A. Jesus tells His disciples to cross to the other side of the lake (see Luke 8:22).
   B. Jesus falls asleep while a storm arises (see Luke 8:23–24).
   C. Jesus rebukes the storm and asks, "Where is your faith?" (Luke 8:25).

IV. Jesus went into a storm with His people so He could show them that He was greater than the storm.
   A. Life is full of storms, but our storms are full of Jesus.
   B. God uses our storms to make a way for us to see His works and His glory.
   C. Our job in the storm is to not lose focus on Jesus and to stay fixated on Him.

V. It's critical for us to remain focused on Jesus during a storm because . . .
   A. Staying focused on Jesus fulfills our purpose (see Colossians 1:16).
      1. Our heart beats because we were made *by* Jesus and *for* Jesus.
      2. We have the *grace* of God *and* a personal relationship with Christ.
   B. Staying focused on Jesus gives us hope in any and every circumstance.
      1. We have hope because we know that Jesus was raised from the dead.
      2. We have the promise that Jesus will make all things right.
   C. Staying focused on Jesus enables our worship of Him to be uninterrupted.
      1. The disciples worshiped Jesus when they saw His power in the storm.
      2. We likewise express *true* worship to Jesus when we witness His power in the storm.

NOTES

Discuss | 35 MINUTES

Discuss what you just watched by answering the following questions.

1. How do you handle the tension between any struggles you may be facing and the cultural expectations to enjoy the Christmas season?

2. How does the idea of "spiritual replacement" resonate with you and your circumstances right now? What does it mean to focus on Jesus without denying the challenges you face?

3. Does Jesus' response— "Where is your faith?"— to His disciples in the midst of a storm-tossed sea surprise you? Why or why not?

4. When you're experiencing the pain and turmoil of life's storms, what gives you perspective? How does your faith in Christ help you weather the storms?

5. Which of the reasons/benefits listed for staying focused on Jesus in the midst of life's storms stand out to you? Why?

Respond | 10 MINUTES

As you close out this session, reflect for a few minutes on past storms you've endured in your life. These may include obvious examples, such as a health crisis, or more subtle ones, like a desire for a closer relationship with God. Use the questions below to aid in your reflection as you consider how God has used your past waiting to fulfill His plans for your life.

- What was the last major storm you've endured in your life?
- Looking back, what can you see now that you couldn't see then?
- How has God used that storm and others to make you stronger and more reliant on Him?
- Does recalling how God has worked in the midst of past storms make it any easier to wait on Him presently? Why or why not?

Pray | 10 MINUTES

God's Word reminds us, "Let us then with confidence draw near to the throne of grace, that we may receive mercy and find grace to help in time of need" (Hebrews 4:16 ESV). Praying for one another in the midst of our waiting helps us experience community, connection, and compassion. We feel less alone when we know that others are lifting up our worries. So pray together as you close your group, and then share any requests as you feel led. Use the space below to write any requests mentioned so you can pray for them in the week ahead.

Name   Request

Personal Study

In the previous session, we discussed the frustration we sometimes experience while waiting on God to move, guide, reveal, provide, or heal. What we tend to overlook is that God continues to work on our behalf during these seasons, even if we're unable to see it or feel it in the ways we would like. During such stormy times, we learn to exercise faith by focusing on Jesus rather than the blinders of our circumstances. As you work through the exercises in this week's personal study, be sure to write down your responses to the questions. If you are reading the *Waiting Here for You* devotional alongside this study, make sure you're caught up from the first week before continuing. Use the daily reading schedule to help you stay on track.

Weekly Reading Plan

Before You Begin	Read "Seek and You Will Find" (page 38) and "Compassion Over Consumption" (page 42)
Day 1	Complete Study 1 and read "Whom Shall I Fear" (page 46)
Day 2	Complete Study 2 and read "God Will Make a Way" (page 50)
Day 3	Complete Study 3 and read "Glory in the Highest" (page 54)
Day 4	Go through the Connect & Discuss questions with a friend or someone in the group and read "Hope When We Can't Hold On" (page 58)
Day 5	Complete the Worship While You Wait exercises and read "Be Still" (page 62)
Before Next Week	Read "In The Valley of Death, You Are There" (page 66) and "Compassion Over Consumption" (page 70)

Waiting Is Never Wasted

On average, it takes twenty-one days for a chick to be hatched from an egg. When the moment finally arrives for the chick to be hatched, it happens in two stages. First, the chick will poke a small hole in the shell (known as "pipping"). Next, the chick will slowly make that hole larger (known as "unzipping"). The process can take hours—sometimes more than twenty-four hours. But this period of waiting and struggle is necessary for the chick to develop into a healthy chicken. Rush the process, and the chick is likely to die.

Waiting on God to work in our lives will often take a similar course. For days and weeks, it may seem as if nothing is happening. When we do finally see some progress, it can lead to another set of delays. But during these seasons, we need to recognize that God never wastes times of waiting but uses them to strengthen and develop us. He may not give us the future glimpses or felt assurance we long to have, but we can still trust Him, standing firm on the promises of His Word. As Paul states, "And we know that in all things God works for the good of those who love him, who have been called according to his purpose" (Romans 8:28).

One person in the Bible who knew all about waiting was Joseph. Sold into slavery by his jealous older brothers, Joseph endured betrayal, bondage, false accusations, and imprisonment in a foreign culture until eventually landing before the Egyptian pharaoh. Finally, Joseph's interpretive and prophetic gifts were recognized and put to use for maximum impact. A famine in Israel sent Joseph's brothers searching for food, where they soon learned what became of their betrayed brother. Now he was in a position of power and authority over them. How would Joseph respond after all these years? As you read his response below, notice what he mentioned as his focus:

> When Joseph's brothers saw that their father was dead, they said, "What if Joseph holds a grudge against us and pays us back for all the wrongs we did to him?" So they sent word to Joseph, saying, "Your father left these instructions before he died: 'This is what you are to say to Joseph: I ask you to forgive your brothers the sins and the wrongs they committed in treating you so badly.' Now please forgive the sins of the servants of the God of your father." When their message came to him, Joseph wept.

His brothers then came and threw themselves down before him. "We are your slaves," they said.

But Joseph said to them, "Don't be afraid. Am I in the place of God? You intended to harm me, but God intended it for good to accomplish what is now being done, the saving of many lives. So then, don't be afraid. I will provide for you and your children." And he reassured them and spoke kindly to them.

GENESIS 50:15–21

1. Why do you suppose Joseph wept when he received the message his brothers sent him? How would you have felt if you were in his place?

2. Joseph had an opportunity to take revenge on his brothers, but what did he focus on instead? What allowed him to see God at work through so many trials and storms?

3. The Hebrew migration to Egypt ultimately led to their bondage. This set up their deliverance with Moses as their leader—chosen and empowered by God. Similarly, what events do you look back on in your own life that reveal a trail of God's divine purposes?

4. Paul writes that "in all things God works for the good of those who love him" (Romans 8:28). What are some situations in your life that are hard for you to see as bringing about any good? What storms have you endured that don't seem to reveal God's goodness?

5. In which areas of your life are you waiting on Jesus to calm the winds and waves? How can you keep faith in His ability to provide what you're waiting on?

Father, bring me through the
fire and rising tide. You have
given the Holy Christ in exchange
for my life. Will You not also,
with Him, freely give me all things?
I am clinging to You and waiting
in expectation. Don't let me sink.
Hold on to me. Amen.

Hurry Up and Wait

People in certain fields and industries, often entertainment and media, talk about projects that require them to "hurry up and wait." For example, movies are often filmed and then not released for years. Editing and post-production take time, finding a distributor can be time-consuming, and then comes marketing and all the efforts that go into promoting the launch. The collaborative process required before a film or television series gets made is equally as start-stop, requiring the right mix of financing, scheduling actors and production team members, finding locations, and building sets. Once there is a green light, then there's a rush to get it finished so it can be available for viewing as quickly as possible, thus the ongoing cycles of rushing to wait.

David experienced this same kind of delay. After he was anointed by Samuel (see 1 Samuel 16:13), he waited about fifteen years before becoming king of Israel (see 2 Samuel 5:3–5). During that interval, David didn't passively wait or complain about why he couldn't begin his reign. Instead, he respected that his predecessor, King Saul, was still on the throne and that God's timing would determine when it was his turn. The shepherd from Bethlehem knew he had been chosen and anointed by God for an enormous position of leadership, and as he grew into adulthood, he accepted that the Lord was preparing him for this role. All the battles, relationships, life-threatening situations, and political turmoil equipped David in ways necessary for him to lead God's people.

We often find ourselves in these same kinds of in-between times. God reveals a direction for our lives and gives us a clear and strong sense of our purpose. And then . . . nothing seems to happen for weeks, months, years. We're confident that God has called us and is guiding us, but we're forced to accept that we need more time to fulfill that calling. Trusting God sometimes requires us to hurry up and wait, but our waiting is never wasted. During those intervals, we learn to rely more fully on God's Spirit and to use the gifts, abilities, and resources stewarded to us.

> But the Lord said to Samuel, "Do not consider his appearance or his height, for I have rejected him. The Lord does not look at the things people look at. People look at the outward appearance, but the Lord looks at the heart." . . .
>   "There is still the youngest," Jesse answered. "He is tending the sheep."
>   Samuel said, "Send for him; we will not sit down until he arrives."
>   So he sent for him and had him brought in. He was glowing with health and had a fine appearance and handsome features.
>   Then the Lord said, "Rise and anoint him; this is the one."

So Samuel took the horn of oil and anointed him in the presence of his brothers, and from that day on the Spirit of the LORD came powerfully upon David. Samuel then went to Ramah.

1 SAMUEL 16:7, 11–13

All the tribes of Israel came to David at Hebron and said, "We are your own flesh and blood. In the past, while Saul was king over us, you were the one who led Israel on their military campaigns. And the LORD said to you, 'You will shepherd my people Israel, and you will become their ruler.'"

When all the elders of Israel had come to King David at Hebron, the king made a covenant with them at Hebron before the LORD, and they anointed David king over Israel.

David was thirty years old when he became king, and he reigned forty years. In Hebron he reigned over Judah seven years and six months, and in Jerusalem he reigned over all Israel and Judah thirty-three years.

2 SAMUEL 5:1–5

1. What are you waiting on God to fulfill that you know He has already started in your life? How long have you been waiting since you realized His calling or direction for this?

2. In your Bible, do a quick read through 1 Samuel 16 and 2 Samuel 5. List below the events and situations that David encountered in between his anointing and ascending to the throne of Israel that particularly stand out to you. Next to each item you list, write down how it likely prepared David for his forty-year reign.

Situation or Event

How It Prepared David to Be King

_____

_____

_____

_____

_____

_____

_____

_____

_____

_____

_____

_____

3. How do you think God has been preparing you during this time of waiting? What have you learned so far that will help you fulfill your purpose with more impact?

4. Based on all David experienced between his anointing and his appointing, what can you learn from the way he handled waiting on God to fulfill His promise?

5. What delays, obstacles, and barriers have you encountered or continue to face as you wait for God's timing? How can moving through them with confidence deepen your faith?

Delayed Gratification

Each year, the beginning of the Christmas season seems to start a little earlier. You've probably noticed how online retailers, stores, and advertisers begin urging you to start shopping back in October—or sometimes even earlier! The bottom line is more often the main motivator of this, but in reality many people love to rush into Christmas as soon as possible. They enjoy the special traditions, decorations, and festivites so much that they eagerly embrace any opportunity to suspend the mundane normalcy of life. Maybe this is you.

Or, you might be the person who resists the pressure to begin the Christmas holiday season so soon. Rather than getting caught up in extending the season, you may be tempted to wait before getting in the Christmas spirit—especially if you're anticipating a feeling of heaviness around December 25. Depending on your circumstances and what you're waiting on, you may not feel any of the peace, joy, or hope promised by holiday cards and well-wishers.

Whether you're jumping in early or dragging your feet this year, it's hard to escape the sense of delayed gratification associated with Christmas. You look ahead, make plans and lists, arrange schedules, connect with friends and family, shop and wrap, plan meals and cook. The big day arrives . . . then, just like that, it is over until next year. And in all the planning and anticipation, it is easy to get caught up in the busyness of it all and miss the true meaning of why you are celebrating in the first place. This is why understanding Advent as a season of waiting can make such a transformational difference in your life even after Christmas has come and gone.

1. Where is your head and heart this year as Christmas approaches? Take a moment to consider each of the following statements and respond with whether you agree or disagree.

I am very excited about Christmas this year and am looking forward to it.

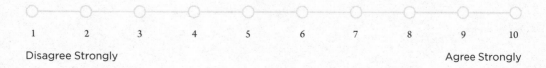

| 1 | 2 | 3 | 4 | 5 | 6 | 7 | 8 | 9 | 10 |

Disagree Strongly   Agree Strongly

Thinking about all that needs to get done before Christmas is overwhelming.

| 1 | 2 | 3 | 4 | 5 | 6 | 7 | 8 | 9 | 10 |

Disagree Strongly   Agree Strongly

I want to feel more excited about Christmas than I am feeling about it now.

| 1 | 2 | 3 | 4 | 5 | 6 | 7 | 8 | 9 | 10 |

Disagree Strongly   Agree Strongly

I don't look forward to Christmas as much now as I did in the past.

| 1 | 2 | 3 | 4 | 5 | 6 | 7 | 8 | 9 | 10 |

Disagree Strongly   Agree Strongly

2. When have you waited on something that proved worth the wait?

3. Do you struggle with waiting for gratification in your daily life or does it seem to come naturally? How does the way you consider attaining what you want—now versus later—affect the way you wait on God to move in your life?

Then the word of the Lord came to him: "This man will not be your heir, but a son who is your own flesh and blood will be your heir." He took him outside and said, "Look up at the sky and count the stars—if indeed you can count them." Then he said to him, "So shall your offspring be."

GENESIS 15:4–5

God also said to Abraham . . . "I will bless her and will surely give you a son by her. I will bless her so that she will be the mother of nations; kings of peoples will come from her." Abraham fell facedown; he laughed and said to himself, "Will a son be born to a man a hundred years old? Will Sarah bear a child at the age of ninety?"

GENESIS 17:15–17

4. God made a covenant with Abraham, promising him a child with his wife Sarah—a son who would become the first of countless generations descended from Abraham. As years passed without conceiving, Abraham and Sarah surely wondered how God would fulfill His promise. Abraham even fell facedown laughing when God reassured him this promise would be kept. When have you experienced assurance from God for something that seemed humanly impossible? How did you respond as time passed without receiving what you knew God had promised you?

> Now the Lᴏʀᴅ was gracious to Sarah as he had said, and the Lᴏʀᴅ did for Sarah what he had promised. Sarah became pregnant and bore a son to Abraham in his old age, at the very time God had promised him. Abraham gave the name Isaac to the son Sarah bore him. When his son Isaac was eight days old, Abraham circumcised him, as God commanded him. Abraham was a hundred years old when his son Isaac was born to him.
>
> **GENESIS 21:1–5**

5. Despite their advanced ages, Abraham and Sarah received the gift of a son as promised by the Lord. The name they chose, Isaac, means "he laughs" or "he will laugh," reflecting both their struggle to believe the seemingly impossible as well as their celebratory joy. Think about the situation you just identified where God provided something that seemed humanly impossible. How did you respond when you received this gift from the Lord?

Connect & Discuss

Take some time today to connect with someone and share how you have experienced God working even in the midst of your waiting. If you're part of a group completing this study, reach out to a fellow group member and discuss some of your insights from this week's session. Use any of the following prompts to help begin your time of sharing and waiting together.

When have you seen God working while you waited? What was the outcome of realizing He had a bigger purpose in mind than you could see at the time?

How has God used your times of waiting to help and encourage others in their times of waiting?

Why are we encouraged when we realize we're not the only ones waiting on God to work in our lives? How does waiting together create a bond among people and strengthen community?

How do you sense God is working in your life as you wait on Christmas?

What struck you in your personal studies this week about how you view God while you wait? How has your perspective changed since starting this study?

How can you pray for one another as you continue experiencing this season of Advent?

Worship While You Wait

Set aside about fifteen minutes today to worship and connect with God without interruption or distractions. If you're using an Advent wreath, light two candles (one for each week) and turn off the other lights in the room. Or simply light a couple of your own holiday candles as you sit in a dark or dimly lit spot. Notice how you see your surroundings differently when illuminated by candlelight. Consider what you can smell in the room, like the scent of your Christmas tree or the fresh greenery around your wreath.

Now close your eyes and take a few moments to simply focus on your breathing and how your body feels right now. Let yourself relax and release physical areas of your body that seem tense or agitated. Try to hit pause on all the thoughts and to-do lists spinning in your mind. While it may feel like you're "doing nothing" right now, consider how this time of worship can enhance the rhythm of your day and your anticipation of Christmas.

As you move into a time of prayer, praise, and worship, use the questions and prompts below to help you focus. Feel free to diverge as the Spirit leads, but try not to zone out or get caught up in thinking about what's ahead in the rest of your day or week.

Is there anything causing you stress or angst today? Think about each situation, relationship, need, or concern, and imagine handing them over to God as you open your heart and still yourself before Him. Try to focus on allowing God to meet you right where you are in this moment.

What are some areas of uncertainty or confusion in your life right now that you would like God to illuminate? Do you want Him to provide healing, cleansing, clarity, direction, reassurance—or something else?

As you reflect on this past week's personal studies, what has connected with you? How has God used these studies to reveal more of Himself to you?

Spend a few minutes in prayer, asking God to help you trust Him with all that He's doing in your life that you are unable to comprehend. Write down anything that you sense He is revealing to you.

Once He came in blessing,
All our sins redressing;
Came in likeness lowly,
Son of God most holy;
Bore the cross to save us;
Hope and freedom gave us.
Come, then, O Lord Jesus,
From our sins release us.
Keep our hearts believing,
That we, grace receiving,
Ever may confess You
Till in heav'n we bless You.

"ONCE HE CAME IN BLESSING"
JOHANN ROH (1487–1547)

Session Three

Waiting on God and with God

I waited patiently for the LORD; he turned to me and heard my cry. He lifted me out of the slimy pit, out of the mud and mire; he set my feet on a rock and gave me a firm place to stand.

PSALM 40:1–2

Welcome | READ ON YOUR OWN

When you are waiting on God to work in your life, you may feel alone as well as lonely. There is a difference. Feelings of being alone are trigged when you are physically separated from other human beings. Feelings of loneliness, on the other hand, can be triggered even when there are other people around you. Simply put, being alone can be described as a physical state, while being lonely is an emotional state.

According to a number of experts, loneliness has reached an epidemic level and is having a devastating impact on physical, mental, and emotional health. Technology, despite its many benefits, is a significant contributor to this problem. Thanks to email, texts, websites, and social media, people no longer have to interact with other humans in person. We can do just about everything virtually—shop, work, date, socialize, study, and visit with doctors and medical experts. While more convenient and efficient, perhaps something essential is lost. We are made for connection with other people—and with God.

Loneliness often increases during the holidays. The media images of families and friends celebrating can trigger feelings of loneliness if the picture-perfect scenes do not match the reality in our lives. We feel that something is missing in our connections with others or that our relationships don't "match up" with what we see. But it is at these times we need to remind ourselves that we are never truly alone. As we read in the Bible, "God has said, 'Never will I leave you; never will I forsake you'" (Hebrews 13:5).

This truth especially resonates at Christmas, because the birth of Jesus demonstrates God's willingness to take on human form. He became Emmanuel, "God with us." No matter how lonely you feel in your waiting, you are not alone. Even as you wait on God, He is with you.

Connect | 15 MINUTES

Start your group session by discussing each of these questions together:

- How do you most enjoy connecting with others during the Christmas season?

- When have you recently battled loneliness?

Watch | 20 MINUTES

Now watch the video for this session. Below is an outline of the key points covered during the teaching. Note any key concepts that stand out to you.

OUTLINE

I. During seasons of waiting, we must remember that God is still working.
   A. God always has a purpose and is doing something important in the wait.
   B. God took His time and created the world in six days—not just six seconds.
   C. Jesus lived on earth for 30 years, waiting, before He started His ministry.
II. God is not in a hurry, and He has higher plans for our lives than we do.
   A. The Westminster Catechism states: "The chief end of man is to glorify God and enjoy him forever."
   B. Our chief aim is often "how do I feel?" and "how do I get what I want?"
   C. We will not be satisfied with such pursuits, which is why God calls us to something much greater.
III. The Israelites' crossing the Red Sea reveals how God works while we wait.
   A. The people had been released after 400 years in Egypt (see Exodus 13:17–18).
   B. Moses and the people took the bones of Joseph with them (see 13:19).
   C. Joseph had faith that God would bring him back to the promised land.
IV. God sometimes leads us the long way to show His sufficiency in our lives.
   A. God could have brought the people into the promised land in two weeks.
   B. But God led them to a dead end at the Red Sea and into the wilderness.
   C. God demonstrated that He was their defender from behind and their deliverer moving forward.
V. God sometimes leads us the long way to convince us that He is always with us.
   A. While we are waiting *on* the Lord, we are also waiting *with* the Lord.
   B. We can travel in the darkness, in the light, in any situation, because God is with us.
   C. God revealed that He is with us when He sent Emmanuel into this world.
VI. God sometimes leads us the long way to reveal to us that He is enough.
   A. Great anthems are not born on the mountaintops but in the valleys of life.
   B. The Israelites' lament on one side of the Red Sea turned into worship on the other side.
   C. We have to worship while we wait because worship keeps our view on Jesus.

NOTES

Discuss | 35 MINUTES

Discuss what you just watched by answering the following questions.

1. Why do you suppose God takes His time rather than immediately answering our requests or moving in our lives? What have you learned about God's character by having to wait on Him?

2. How does having to wait on God's timing point us to something greater than what we want or how we feel?

3. What stands out to you when you consider the way people in the Bible, such as Jacob's son Joseph or the Israelites in Egypt, had to wait on God to move in their lives? What can you learn from their examples to apply to your own times of waiting?

4. When has God led you the long way through a season of trials or struggles? What did you learn about His sufficiency while going through this season?

5. How do you experience God's presence with you even when you're waiting or taking the long way? How does worshiping in the midst of waiting remind you that God is with you?

Respond | 10 MINUTES

As you close out this session, take a few minutes on your own to consider your awareness of God's presence in the midst of your waiting. Throughout the Bible, God states that He is always with you (see Deuteronomy 31:6–8; Joshua 1:5; Matthew 28:20; Hebrews 13:5). In the midst of your waiting on God, you may be tempted to distance yourself until He delivers what you're waiting on. But becoming more aware of His presence as you wait provides an incredible opportunity to draw closer to Him. It enables you to focus on who He is, consider His larger perspective, and rely on His sufficiency as more than enough even while you are waiting.

- How has God been revealing His presence in your life in the midst of your waiting?
- What are some of the benefits of being with God even while waiting on Him?
- What qualities or attributes of God's character stand out to you right now? Why?
- How can you practically draw closer to God during this Advent time of waiting?

Pray | 10 MINUTES

As you close this session, ask God to reveal that He is with you in the midst of your waiting. Thank Him for sustaining you and providing for your needs, even as you face challenges in your life. Ask that He will continue to make you aware of who He is and how He's at work in your daily life. Finally, use the space below to write down any requests so you and your group members can continue to pray about them in the week ahead.

Name   Request

Personal Study

In the previous session, we talked about how God is with us even while we wait on Him. Although we sometimes grow impatient while waiting, we also have an opportunity to know God more intimately. Rather than viewing Him as a holy problem solver or provider, we can choose to use our time waiting to get to know Him better. Making the most of relational opportunity requires a shift in perspective, one that requires you to be focused on the present moment, not pausing now to focus on what you hope happens in the future. As you work through the exercises in this week's personal studies, continue to write down your responses. If you are reading the *Waiting Here for You* devotional, first catch up with all readings from the second week. Use the daily reading schedule to help you stay on track.

Weekly Reading Plan

Before You Begin	Read "In the Valley of Death, You Are There" (page 66) and "Compassion Over Consumption" (page 70)
Day 1	Complete Study 1 and read "God Gives All Good Things" (page 74)
Day 2	Complete Study 2 and read "Where Our Song Comes From" (page 78)
Day 3	Complete Study 3 and read "Goodbye Condemnation" (page 82)
Day 4	Go through the Connect & Discuss questions with a friend or someone in the group and read "Don't Count God Out" (page 86)
Day 5	Complete the Worship While You Wait exercises and read "Jesus Is Our Feast" (page 90)
Before Next Week	Read "Not Yet Home" (page 94) and "Compassion Over Consumption" (page 98)

Study One

Count Your Blessings

Children love to dream about all the presents they will receive at Christmas. They make a list of the toys, treats, and tech items they are hoping to find when they finally get to tear into those wrapped boxes under the tree. Some kids (and adults) even shake the packages to see if they can tell what the gift will be by "hearing" the way the content rattles around inside. As the days pass, it only serves to build childrens' anticipation of that fateful moment when their expectations will either be met or left unfulfilled. Once the wrapping paper comes off, the focus shifts to enjoying the gifts they were actually given.

Once we're adults, our views change. Christmas presents and gift-giving can often seem like both a joyful tradition and a troubling burden—a fun part of celebrating the holidays and a costly obligation necessitated by cultural expectations rather than a spirit of generosity. For most people who celebrate Christmas by exchanging gifts with family, friends, and loved ones, the joy is found in the process of making thoughtful, personal selections and anticipating the surprise and gratitude of recipients.

Sometimes, waiting on God can feel like the anticipation we experience both as kids and adults about to open those Christmas gifts. Will we get what we want . . . something more or less than what we expect? When God surprises or overwhelms us with His gifts, it's easy to stop and thank Him. But learning to recognize what He has already given us should require the same intentional gratitude.

Counting your blessings can be a gift that draws you to God's presence and provision where you are right now. Instead of focusing on what's ahead and if you will receive what you want, gratitude for where you are and what you already have can change the way you view the process of waiting. By noticing all that God has done to get you to your current place and how He continues to meet your needs, you realize He hasn't forgotten or failed you.

Yes, you may be in desperate need of what you're waiting on—positive results from a medical test, an annual bonus from work, repair to a broken relationship—but you also have what you need today. Giving thanks for present blessings allows you to recognize that God is *with* you right now—even while waiting *on* Him.

> Rejoice in the Lord always. I will say it again: Rejoice! Let your gentleness be evident to all. The Lord is near. Do not be anxious about anything, but in every situation, by prayer and petition, with thanksgiving, present your requests to God. And the peace of God, which transcends all understanding, will guard your hearts and your minds in Christ Jesus.
>
> **PHILIPPIANS 4:4–7**

1. Many of us experience anxiety during times of uncertainty, when seasons of waiting lead us to anticipate both best-case and worst-case scenarios. While anxious feelings can be a normal response when life seems out of control, we don't have to stay there. According to the above passage, what's the solution to anxiety?

2. What are the benefits of seeking God through prayer and petition? How does time spent with Him in prayer help you experience that "the Lord is near"?

> Shout for joy to the Lord, all the earth.
>   Worship the Lord with gladness;
>   come before him with joyful songs.
> Know that the Lord is God.
>   It is he who made us, and we are his;
>   we are his people, the sheep of his pasture.
> Enter his gates with thanksgiving
>   and his courts with praise;
>   give thanks to him and praise his name.

> For the LORD is good and his love endures forever;
>   his faithfulness continues through all generations.
>
> **PSALM 100:1–5**

3. Shouting for joy and giving God thanks may not be your default response in the midst of waiting on Him. But worship and gratitude take the focus off what you want from God and how you feel about not having received it yet. It shifts your attention to who God is and what it means to "know that the Lord is God." Why is it important to remember that "the Lord is good and his love endures forever" during times of waiting?

4. The psalmist focuses on our relationship with God—He is the Lord and we are His people—as the basis for worshiping and praising Him. What can cause you to lose sight of God's goodness and presence in your life during seasons of waiting? How does worship and praise remind you of who God is and who you are?

5. During the Christmas season, with so much emphasis on spending and consuming, it helps to keep your focus on how God has already blessed you. So today, spend a few minutes listing what you're grateful for. Feel free to start with big items, like your home or your family, but then narrow your focus to those that are particularly personal, such as getting to spend time with an old friend unexpectedly or receiving a surprise gift from a neighbor. Once you've listed as many items as you can, spend another couple minutes reviewing these blessings and thanking God for each one.

Father, give me rest today knowing that when I walk with You, I will never miss out on anything. Give me the grace to do my best, but give me the peace that comes from knowing every good thing comes from You. Amen.

Study Two
Divine Appointments

Perhaps you've heard it said, "There are no coincidences—only evidence of God's perfect timing." Or you may be familiar with, "God may not arrive when you want Him to, but He's always on time." As well intended as these sayings might be, they are rarely helpful when you are in the midst of a crisis and are waiting on God to provide. Yet even when you feel like life is on hold until God reveals your next steps, you can find comfort and peace in His timing.

We mark time in linear form moving forward—counting seconds, minutes, hours, and days—but God exists outside our temporal system. In the New Testament, two different Greek words are used to mark these different expressions of time. The word *cronos* refers to measuring time by human standards. It appears in English words such as *chronology* (the study of time) and *synchronise* (to make something happen at the same time). *Chronos* denotes the passing of time from day to night, from winter into spring, from summer into fall.

The Greek word *kairos*, however, takes a different view of time—one that is based on what is opportune, appropriate, and divinely appointed. The term usually reflects the way a variety of factors and variables come together to reveal God's timing.

In fact, the birth of Jesus may be the best illustration of *kairos* timing. After 400 years of silence, God chose the perfect and right time for His Son to be born in Bethlehem. Luke's account of Jesus' birth begins, "It came to pass in those days" (2:1 NKJV), and then reveals, "So it was, that while they were there, the days were completed for her to be delivered" (verse 6 NKJV).

When we're waiting on God, we're relying on His divine, all-knowing, perfect sense of timing. We may not understand it, and we may not like it, but we learn to trust that His ways are not our ways and that His relationship to time transcends our mortal understanding and perspective on it. If we can trust God, we can also trust in His timing.

Best of all, God's *kairos* is always present in our *chronos*. He is with us right now—at this very moment—as we wait for Him to choose the best time to fulfill what we're waiting for.

1. When have you experienced God's *kairos* time in your life—an opportunity or coincidence that could only have been divinely orchestrated and synchronized?

The beginning of the good news about Jesus the Messiah, the Son of God, as it is written in Isaiah the prophet:

"I will send my messenger ahead of you,
    who will prepare your way"—
"a voice of one calling in the wilderness,
    'Prepare the way for the Lord,
    make straight paths for him.'"

And so John the Baptist appeared in the wilderness, preaching a baptism of repentance for the forgiveness of sins. . . .

After John was put in prison, Jesus went into Galilee, proclaiming the good news of God. "The time has come," he said. "The kingdom of God has come near. Repent and believe the good news!"

MARK 1:1–4, 14–15

2. Before Mark tells us that John the Baptist started preaching a baptism of repentance, he refers to Isaiah's prophecies about the Messiah hundreds of years before. This connection emphasizes the way God's timing (*kairos*) had finally burst into the right time in earthly

history (*chronos*). Why do you think God used prophets and John the Baptist to foretell the coming of Jesus, the Messiah? How do they reveal the intersection of *kairos* and *chronos*?

3. After getting baptized, fasting for forty days in the desert, and being tempted by Satan, Jesus began "proclaiming the good news of God" by announcing "the time had come. . . . The kingdom of God has come near" (verses 14–15). Why was it important for Jesus to be baptized by John, fast in the desert, and be tempted by the Enemy before proclaiming the gospel publicly? How did these events prepare Christ for all He experienced afterward?

Be very careful, then, how you live—not as unwise but as wise, making the most of every opportunity, because the days are evil. Therefore do not be foolish, but understand what the Lord's will is. Do not get drunk on wine, which leads to debauchery. Instead, be filled with the Spirit, speaking to one another with psalms, hymns, and songs from the Spirit. Sing and make music from your heart to the Lord, always giving thanks to God the Father for everything, in the name of our Lord Jesus Christ.

EPHESIANS 5:15–20

4. Paul urges the believers in Ephesus to "make the most of every opportunity, because the days are evil." He references *kairos* time here, and other translations render this with more direct temporal language: "making the best use of the time" (ESV) or "redeeming the time" (NKJV). What does it mean for you to make the best use of your time from a *kairos*, or eternal, perspective? How does this change the way you view your waiting periods?

5. Paul concludes his exhortation here by emphasizing the importance of "always giving thanks to God the Father for everything, in the name of our Lord Jesus Christ." Once again, we see that maintaining an ongoing sense of gratitude helps keep us grounded at all times—even in uncertain, scary times when we're waiting on God to deliver us. How does thanking, praising, and worshiping God take us outside of *chronos* time? How does this shift allow us to experience more patience as we realize God is with us as we wait?

Wait with Wonder

You might be familiar with the American folk hymn "I Wonder as I Wander" that's often sung at Christmastime. Its simple melody and plaintive lyrics offer a moody meditation on the fact that Jesus came to earth in human form to die. The song reminds us that when we focus on the birth of Jesus without remembering why He came, we're cutting short the story of "God with us."

But the song also subtly reminds us that the fact that Jesus came to die for "poor on'ry people like you and like I" should evoke a sense of wonder—a reflection on the sobering aspect of Christ's birth. The kind of wonder based on awe, on unexpected surprise, on the miraculous and marvelous. Maintaining awareness of Jesus' purpose in coming also helps us remain aware of God's presence in the midst of our waiting.

Without knowing the Easter story that would unfold thirty-three years after that baby was born, the miracle of Christmas is incomplete. God was not only with us in human form—He was also willing to die for our sins and then overcome death by rising from the tomb. He was willing to give us the gift of the Holy Spirit so that He could dwell in us all the time. The Easter part of the story may seem uncomfortable compared to the pastoral scene of shepherds being visited by angels with the good news of Christ's birth. But the cross completes what began with the manger and extends God's relentless grace and mercy to us right where we are.

So, while you're waiting on God to complete what He has started, don't forget to wonder. In fact, experiencing wonder while you wait prevents your heart from wandering—from losing hope and drifting away from your relationship with God. Even during those times when you may wander, God is still with you.

> God sent the angel Gabriel to Nazareth, a town in Galilee, to a virgin pledged to be married to a man named Joseph, a descendant of David. The virgin's name was Mary. The angel went to her and said, "Greetings, you who are highly favored! The Lord is with you."
>
> Mary was greatly troubled at his words and wondered what kind of greeting this might be. But the angel said to her, "Do not be afraid, Mary; you have

found favor with God. You will conceive and give birth to a son, and you are to call him Jesus. He will be great and will be called the Son of the Most High. The Lord God will give him the throne of his father David, and he will reign over Jacob's descendants forever; his kingdom will never end."

"How will this be," Mary asked the angel, "since I am a virgin?"

The angel answered, "The Holy Spirit will come on you, and the power of the Most High will overshadow you. So the holy one to be born will be called the Son of God. Even Elizabeth your relative is going to have a child in her old age, and she who was said to be unable to conceive is in her sixth month. For no word from God will ever fail."

"I am the Lord's servant," Mary answered. "May your word to me be fulfilled." Then the angel left her.

LUKE 1:26–38

1. Mary was one of the first people on earth to discover how God was going to fulfill His promise to send a Savior. Rather than allow fear to prevent her from taking this step of faith, Mary chose to accept God's invitation with wonder. What stands out to you about Mary's response in her startling conversation with Gabriel? How do you suppose she was able to shift from being "greatly troubled" to stating, "I am the Lord's servant"?

2. The only question that Mary asked focuses on her human understanding of how pregnancy works: "How will this be since I am a virgin?" Gabriel's explanation provided an answer but remained mysterious. Still, Mary accepted the vital role offered to her as the

mother of the Messiah. What other questions do you imagine Mary might have had running through her mind at the time? What questions would you have wanted to ask Gabriel if you were in her place?

"My soul glorifies the Lord
　　and my spirit rejoices in God my Savior,
for he has been mindful
　　of the humble state of his servant.
From now on all generations will call me blessed,
　　for the Mighty One has done great things for me—
　　holy is his name.
His mercy extends to those who fear him,
　　from generation to generation.
He has performed mighty deeds with his arm;
　　he has scattered those who are proud in their inmost thoughts.
He has brought down rulers from their thrones
　　but has lifted up the humble.
He has filled the hungry with good things
　　but has sent the rich away empty.
He has helped his servant Israel,
　　remembering to be merciful
to Abraham and his descendants forever,
　　just as he promised our ancestors."

LUKE 1:46–55

3. Known as "Mary's song" or the "Magnificat," this poetic monologue reveals Mary's response to being chosen by God. Notice the way she thanks and praises God both for what He has done for her as well as what He has done for all humankind. Where do you see Mary expressing wonder in her song? How do these feelings lead her to worship and praise God?

4. Mary expressed her song after she was pregnant—a season of physical and natal growth that definitely requires waiting. How does expressing her wonder and joy ground her in the present, even as she anticipates giving birth in the very near future?

5. As you consider where you are in the midst of waiting, as well as how you sense God's presence right now, what would you write to express your thoughts and feelings? What would your song of wonder be? It doesn't have to be poetic, but it should be honest.

Connect & Discuss

Waiting can be lonely for people—particularly during the holiday season. This is why reaching out to others who are on their own during this season can be an act of God's compassion among His people. Today, make it a point to connect with someone and hear how he or she is doing with Christmas being almost a week away. Or, if you're part of a group completing this study, reach out to another group member and share how you've been experiencing God with you while you're waiting on Him for more. Use any of the following prompts to help begin your time of sharing together.

How is your experience of Christmas different this year than the last few?

How have you experienced God in your life this past week? What does this reveal about how He cares for you even while you're waiting on His healing, provision, resolution, or guidance?

What is one of God's promises that means a lot to you right now? How does it remind you that He is with you even if you're feeling lonely, exhausted, impatient, or overwhelmed?

What's a favorite family tradition or part of celebrating Christmas that you're especially looking forward to this year? Why?

What has God shown you or taught you this week that changes the way you think about waiting?

How can you pray for one another in the midst of waiting this Advent?

Worship While You Wait

What would celebrating Christmas be without music? While you may already be experiencing holiday-music fatigue after hearing it non-stop wherever you go, the power of Christmas carols, hymns, and songs remains significant as a vital part of worship. You likely have a few favorites that you never tire of hearing or that have special significance based on past memories. Today as you worship while you wait, incorporate one of these personal favorites as a way of slowing down, focusing your attention on God's presence, and stilling your heart before Him. You may decide to play your song selection to start your worship time or play it later as you reflect and pray.

As with previous weeks, choose a time and place without interruptions or distractions for at least fifteen minutes. If you're using an Advent wreath to mark each week, light three candles. Traditionally, the candle for the third week differs in color from the others. While each candle in the Advent wreath symbolically represents a different quality or perspective related to the birth of Christ, the third week's candle usually differs in color—often pink instead of purple or white. The difference in color emphasizes joy, particularly the joy experienced by the shepherds when they received the news of the angel and proceeded to find Jesus in the manger, just as they had been told.

The basis for the shepherds' joy is cause for your joy as well. Jesus chose to lower Himself and become human, fully God and fully man. When His work on earth was complete, Jesus ascended back to heaven but sent the gift of the Holy Spirit to dwell among and in His people. No matter what you may be waiting on or experiencing right now, God is with you.

> With Christmas quickly approaching, think about what's currently weighing on your mind and heart. Without getting lost in your thoughts or concerns, let them pass through your mind as you hand them over to God and shift your attention to Him.

As you enjoy the music you selected, consider why you chose it. Take some time to listen closely to the lyrics and thank God for the gift of Jesus. How does the song remind you of God's presence in your life?

Think back on this past week and your experience completing the personal studies. What lingers with you and resonates the most? What does it mean for God to be with you even as you wait on Him?

Spend a few minutes in prayer, recalling all the blessings God has given you today. Thank Him for who He is and for His willingness to be there with you at this very moment. Listen for anything He wants to tell you or show you.

My Savior paid the debt I owe

And for my sin was smitten;

Within the Book of Life I know

My name has now been written.

I will not doubt, for I am free

And Satan cannot threaten me;

There is no condemnation!

May Christ our intercessor be

And through His blood and merit

Read from His book that we are free

With all who life inherit.

Then we shall see Him face to face,

With all His saints in that blest place

Which He has purchased for us.

"THE DAY IS SURELY DRAWING NEAR"
BARTHOLOMÄUS RINGWALDT (1532–1599)

Session Four

God Is Waiting for You

So the LORD *must wait for you to come to him so he can show you his love and compassion. For the* LORD *is a faithful God. Blessed are those who wait for his help.*

ISAIAH 30:18 NLT

Welcome | READ ON YOUR OWN

Have you ever made a date with someone only to feel stood up? You're sitting at a restaurant, or waiting in an office, or pacing by a park bench . . . and the person is not there. You text but get no response. You double-check your schedule and scroll through your texts to make sure you didn't make a mistake about the time or place. Then you look up—and the person is standing in front of you. "Where were you?" you hear. "I've been waiting here for you, just like we planned . . ."

In that moment, you realize the misunderstanding. You didn't specify the exact place inside the restaurant, or which meeting room or office, or the specific spot to meet in the park. So while you were waiting on the other person, he or she was doing the same thing and waiting on you. Sometimes when we're waiting on God, we may not realize He's actually already waiting on us. We assume we will recognize His guidance in a particular way but overlook how He reveals Himself to us. We get locked in on our expectations only to discover God loves to surprise us. He lets us know that He's always ahead of us, waiting for us to seek, find, and know Him.

This was true when God sent His Son to earth to be born in what was little more than a cow shed. During those four centuries while the people of Israel waited for God to send the Messiah, they probably assumed His arrival would be unmistakable. You know, lots of royal fanfare and extravagant celebrations at the temple, or perhaps a major battle to take down their latest enemy and restore Israel as a political powerhouse. But God turned their expectations upside down and entered this world in a humble manner. Oh, there was fanfare—heavenly angels proclaiming God's glory—and extravagant gifts from foreign royal dignitaries. But none of it likely met people's expectations. Jesus arrived, but few realized the Savior was in their midst.

God wants us to receive so much more than we expect. He's already ahead of us, using our circumstances, choices, and consequences as He shapes His plans for our lives. No matter what you're waiting for, God is already there, waiting for you.

Connect | 15 MINUTES

Start your group session by discussing each of these questions together:

- What insights on God's character were revealed during last week's personal studies?

- When was the last time you mixed up a meeting time that resulted in someone waiting on you? Explain what happened.

Watch | 20 MINUTES

Now watch the video for this session. Below is an outline of the key points covered during the teaching. Note any key concepts that stand out to you.

OUTLINE

I. In the Christmas story, Augustus Caesar issued a decree, but God had a plan.

    A. Everyone was required to return to their city of origin (see Luke 2:1–3).

    B. There was no arguing his decrees, so Joseph and Mary went to Bethlehem.

    C. People make decrees that disrupt lives, but God always has a plan.

II. Paul writes in 2 Corinthians 4 that we need to trust in God's work while we wait.

    A. The light of God has come through Christ (see verse 6).

    B. Emmanuel now lives in us by the indwelling Spirit of God (see verses 7–11).

    C. Knowing God is transforming us, we do not lose heart (see verses 16–18), viewing our troubles as momentary compared to the eternity that awaits us.

III. By trusting God in the wait, we develop character that produces faithfulness.

    A. We can find joy in our trials when we recognize how God is using them (see James 1:2–4).

    B. There is a reward for those who choose to undergo God's transforming process (see 1 Peter 3–5).

    C. God's objective is not to make our lives easier but to make our lives matter.

IV. By trusting God in the wait, we gain confidence in God's supreme provision.

    A. Trials are not for us to prove that we're enough for God but for God to reveal that He is enough for us.

    B. We can be real and say we are perplexed by what He is doing in the trial.

    C. Failure is not admitting weakness . . . failure is not believing in God's strength.

V. By trusting God in the wait, we minister powerfully to a broken world.

    A. When we see Jesus, we will be glad our trials led to the salvation of others.

    B. When we share the gospel and spread God's love, we invest in eternity.

    C. Others may persecute us, but they cannot overcome the love of God.

VI. By trusting God in the wait, we lay our worship at the feet of Jesus.

    A. The Magi brought gifts of gold, frankincense, and myrrh (see Matthew 2:11).

    B. Jesus will give us a crown when we are before Him on the last day (see James 1:12), representing our trust in God's transformative work in the trials.

    C. All that we will have to offer Jesus on that day is our worship for giving us those trials that we endured.

NOTES

Discuss | 35 MINUTES

Discuss what you just watched by answering the following questions.

1. When have you seen God use someone else's decrees or decisions to bring about His plans for your life? What did you learn from this experience?

2. How has God used past challenges to strengthen your character and deepen your faith? How does going through these experiences allow you to find God while you wait?

3. When have you found joy in the midst of a trial or painful season because you knew God was using it for your good? What's required for you to sustain this joy when waiting?

4. What are some ways God has shown Himself to be enough for you during hard times? How has He provided what you needed to keep going?

5. How does trusting God in the midst of your wait allow you to minister to others? What has God uniquely equipped you to offer to others because of what you've experienced?

Respond | 10 MINUTES

As you close out this final session, take a few minutes to reflect on what you've learned during these past weeks—about waiting, about yourself, about God.

- How has your view of waiting on God changed since you began this study?
- How has observing Advent enriched your experience of Christmas so far?
- What has surprised you most about what you've learned and experienced?
- When have you most recently realized that God was already with you, waiting for you to notice Him?

Pray | 10 MINUTES

As you close your time today, thank God for all you've learned through this study over the past few weeks. Ask that you would continue to wait expectantly and patiently, trusting Him to be with you each moment of each day as you wait on Him to reveal your next steps. Praise Him for loving you enough to send His Son in such a humble, unexpected way for those with eyes to see. Finally, use the spaces below to write down any prayer requests mentioned so that you and your group members can continue to pray about them moving forward.

Name   Request

Personal Study

Congratulations on reaching this final personal study! You've done an amazing job of deepening your relationship with God by using Advent as a way of focusing on what it means to wait *on* God and to wait *with* God. You've likely realized the process of waiting is often a more significant part of your spiritual growth than receiving what you've been waiting on. Even in the midst of challenging times, God wants you to need Him more than any earthly thing that He can provide. He wants you to rest in the certainty that you can never be separated from His love. He wants you to experience a deeper sense of joy and peace that only comes from Him and His Spirit dwelling inside you. Keep these points in mind as you work through this final study. If you are reading the *Waiting Here for You* devotional, first catch up on the readings from the third week. Use the daily reading schedule to help you finish.

Weekly Reading Plan

Before You Begin	Read "Not Yet Home" (page 94) and "Compassion Over Consumption" (page 98)
Day 1	Complete Study 1 and read "No Other Name" (page 102)
Day 2	Complete Study 2 and read "Humility Looks Good on Everyone" (page 106)
Day 3	Complete Study 3 and read "Light of the World" (page 110)
Day 4	Go through the Connect & Discuss questions with a friend or someone in the group and read "Preparing the Way" (page 114)
Day 5	Complete the Worship While You Wait exercises and read "Man's Decree. God's Design" (page 118), "Hope Rising" (page 122), and "A Savior Is Born" (page 126)
After the Study	Read the conclusion of "The Story of Christmas Grace" (pages 131–136)

Study One

Light Show

What would Christmas be without lights? Twinkling lights on trees, houses, and lawn decorations. Candles in windows, flashing or steady, shining in every color. In many neighborhoods, light shows showcase homes competing to outshine the others. During the long, dark nights of winter, the steady glow of flames or bulbs brightens the bleak season. They create a festive ambiance to counter the beginning of a cold, barren time of year.

Christmas lights also remind us of the bright star guiding the Magi, who followed it to Bethlehem, where they found the baby Jesus (see Matthew 2:2, 9). And lights also remind us of the "glory of the Lord [that] shone around" the shepherds when the angel appeared and shared the divine birth announcement (Luke 2:9). When "a great company of the heavenly host" then joined with the angel to sing praise to God, we might wonder if their presence lit up the night sky as well (verse 13).

Yet these lights are mere glimmers compared to the bold declaration that Jesus made during His public ministry. He told His followers, "I am the light of the world. Whoever follows me will never walk in darkness, but will have the light of life" (John 8:12). Similarly, Christ expressed His purpose in coming to earth by once again referencing light: "I have come into the world as a light, so that no one who believes in me should stay in darkness" (12:46).

When we're waiting on God to provide for us and give us direction, we may feel like we're suspended in the darkness of uncertainty. We know what we hope the Lord will do for us, but we also want to trust Him in doing what He knows is ultimately best for us. In such moments, we must remember the dark-dispelling light we long for is already with us. The constant presence of God's Spirit already dwells within our hearts. Even in our darkest moments, God is always present, waiting on us to realize that we can rely on Him as our constant and ultimate source of illumination.

In the beginning was the Word, and the Word was with God, and the Word was God. He was with God in the beginning. Through him all things were made; without him nothing was made that has been made. In him was life, and that life was the light of all mankind. The light shines in the darkness, and the darkness has not overcome it.

JOHN 1:1–5

1. John's Gospel focuses on Jesus in a unique way from the other Gospel accounts. Matthew begins with a genealogy of Jesus. Mark and Luke describe John the Baptist as the forerunner of the Messiah who prepared the way for the gospel message. But John goes way beyond even a big-picture perspective by describing Jesus' presence and purpose as the very Word made flesh—as light and life. How does taking such a different perspective on the life of Jesus complement the accounts in the other Gospels?

2. Why do you suppose John emphasizes that Jesus is the "light of all mankind"—the light which darkness cannot overcome? How does the light of Christ remind you that God is always waiting for you?

"You are the light of the world. A town built on a hill cannot be hidden. Neither do people light a lamp and put it under a bowl. Instead they put it on its stand, and it gives light to everyone in the house. In the same way, let your light shine before others, that they may see your good deeds and glorify your Father in heaven."

MATTHEW 5:14–16

3. Not only is Jesus the light of the world—He tells His followers that "*you* are the light of the world"! Why does Jesus then urge us not to hide or dim His light within us?

4. How have you allowed God to shine His light through you, in words and actions, during this Advent season? How have you recently dispelled darkness with the light of Christ?

5. The psalmist reminds us, "Your word is a lamp for my feet, a light on my path" (Psalm 119:105). How has God's Word illuminated your understanding of waiting as you've completed this study?

Father, You are everlasting;
You are a light for the nations.
Arise and shine in and through me,
for the night grows long. Give me
patience and strength to be faithful
until the light of Your kingdom
fills the sky. By Your grace and
according to Your mercy, open the eyes
of those who walk in darkness.
Help me not be one who constantly
runs into the safety of the light.
Give me boldness to proclaim the light
I have found in You in the darkest places.
Amen.

There He Is

Seeking and finding Jesus is at the heart of the Christmas story. The shepherds were the first to receive the news of Christ's birth, and after their angelic announcement, they wasted no time finding Jesus. "Let's go to Bethlehem and see this thing that has happened, which the Lord has told us about," they said. "So they hurried off and found Mary and Joseph, and the baby, who was lying in the manger" (Luke 2:15–16).

The Magi from the east followed the star to Jerusalem and, after dodging King Herod, went on to Bethlehem. "The star they had seen when it rose went ahead of them until it stopped over the place where the child was. When they saw the star, they were overjoyed" (Matthew 2:9–10). Jesus was likely a toddler by the time the Magi arrived, so He probably didn't have much to say. But if He had delivered a message to the Magi, He very well might have said, "Welcome! I'm glad you found me. I've been waiting on you."

As your Advent journey draws to a close, the hope is that you can hear Jesus sharing the same message with you. You've been on your way to the manger for a long time—for the past few weeks, at least, but likely much longer. You've been longing to experience more in life than you've found so far. More meaning, more purpose, more hope.

Seeing the baby in the manger offers you all those things and more. He's waiting there for you. God in human form, Emmanuel, is right in front of you—and within you. You don't have to try harder or spend more, volunteer more hours, or serve more people. Jesus came to remind you that He is enough. If you're seeking Him, longing to experience a deeper intimacy with Him than you have ever known, it's time.

He is waiting here for you.

> Now Mary stood outside the tomb crying. As she wept, she bent over to look into the tomb and saw two angels in white, seated where Jesus' body had been, one at the head and the other at the foot.
>   They asked her, "Woman, why are you crying?"

"They have taken my Lord away," she said, "and I don't know where they have put him." At this, she turned around and saw Jesus standing there, but she did not realize that it was Jesus.

He asked her, "Woman, why are you crying? Who is it you are looking for?"

Thinking he was the gardener, she said, "Sir, if you have carried him away, tell me where you have put him, and I will get him."

Jesus said to her, "Mary."

She turned toward him and cried out in Aramaic, "Rabboni!" (which means "Teacher").

JOHN 20:11–16

1. More than three decades after the shepherds and Magi found Jesus, He rose from the dead and defeated sin and death once and for all. When His followers (like Mary) came looking for Him, expecting to find His lifeless body, instead they discovered an empty tomb. How did Mary's expectations prevent her from immediately realizing that Christ had risen? What was the impact of seeing Him there alive, waiting for her?

2. When have you experienced the kind of surprise Mary must have felt by discovering that Jesus was waiting on you in a place you didn't expect to find Him—a hospital room, street corner, rehab center, casino, hotel, concert, or ballgame? How did meeting Jesus in such an unexpected place impact your relationship with Him?

Early in the morning, Jesus stood on the shore, but the disciples did not realize that it was Jesus.

He called out to them, "Friends, haven't you any fish?"

"No," they answered.

He said, "Throw your net on the right side of the boat and you will find some." When they did, they were unable to haul the net in because of the large number of fish.

Then the disciple whom Jesus loved said to Peter, "It is the Lord!" As soon as Simon Peter heard him say, "It is the Lord," he wrapped his outer garment around him (for he had taken it off) and jumped into the water. The other disciples followed in the boat, towing the net full of fish, for they were not far from shore, about a hundred yards. When they landed, they saw a fire of burning coals there with fish on it, and some bread.

Jesus said to them, "Bring some of the fish you have just caught." So Simon Peter climbed back into the boat and dragged the net ashore. It was full of large fish, 153, but even with so many the net was not torn. Jesus said to them, "Come and have breakfast." None of the disciples dared ask him, "Who are you?" They knew it was the Lord. Jesus came, took the bread and gave it to them, and did the same with the fish.

JOHN 21:4–13

3. Jesus seemed to have a thing for showing up at unexpected times and places, surprising those seeking Him by meeting them where they were. Keep in mind in this scene Peter had denied knowing Christ three times the same night Jesus was arrested. With such a bitter betrayal between them, their next encounter might have predictably been awkward. But instead, Jesus served His followers and demonstrated His love for, and confidence in, Peter despite those three denials. Are you surprised that Peter seemed so eager to meet Jesus that he immediately jumped out of the boat and swam ashore? Why or why not?

4. How did Jesus' choice of venue and menu demonstrate that He was waiting there for His disciples to find Him? What is significant about Christ's provision of fish, preparation for cooking it over the fire, and willingness to serve it to His followers?

5. When have you discovered a situation where God had clearly gone before you, providing all you needed and preparing for your arrival? How did these circumstances allow you to find God already waiting on you?

Worth the Wait

On Christmas morning, the wait is over. All the shopping and decorating, the baking and cleaning, the wrapping and tagging—whatever you've anticipated to celebrate the birth of Jesus on this day has arrived. Depending on your expectations, the reality of how you spend Christmas Day may or may not be all you hoped.

Opening presents is certainly part of handling expectations. You know it could go one way or another. Perhaps you won't receive the gift you hoped for. Or maybe you get the gift, but it's the wrong size, or not the right color or model.

On the other hand, you may be delightfully surprised. Instead of getting what you put on your wish list, you discover something you truly love—something you didn't know you wanted or needed. These are the gifts that exceed your expectations and add to the joyful anticipation of Christmas now that the wait is over.

While the time of waiting on Christmas is almost over, you may still be waiting on what you hope God will do in your life. As you've learned throughout this study, you can trust that His timing will indeed be worth the wait. He will bring you clarity at just the right time. But even as you wait on God's timing to see what and how things unfold, don't overlook the gifts you've already received from Him—especially the gift of Emmanuel, God with us—God with you, through the birth of that baby in a manger, Jesus Christ.

The next day he [John the Baptist] saw Jesus coming toward him, and said, "Behold, the Lamb of God, who takes away the sin of the world! This is he of whom I said, 'After me comes a man who ranks before me, because he was before me.' I myself did not know him, but for this purpose I came baptizing with water, that he might be revealed to Israel." And John bore witness: "I saw the Spirit descend from heaven like a dove, and it remained on him. I myself did not know him, but he who sent me to baptize with water said to me, 'He on whom you see the Spirit descend and remain, this is he who baptizes with the Holy Spirit.' And I have seen and have borne witness that this is the Son of God."

JOHN 1:29–34 ESV

1. John the Baptist not only announces the arrival of Jesus but also calls Him the Lamb of God who takes away the sin of the world, which would have been considered blasphemous by the Jewish religious leaders. John goes even further by sharing his eyewitness account of seeing the Spirit descend from heaven and remain on Jesus. And not only does Jesus have the Spirit of God, but He baptizes with the Holy Spirit. John's revelations continue to impact our lives today. What strikes you about John's revelations? How do they affect the way you relate to Jesus through the Holy Spirit?

2. How does the presence of God's Spirit in your life reassure you that everything will be okay even in the midst of waiting, struggling, and persevering?

The next day again John was standing with two of his disciples, and he looked at Jesus as he walked by and said, "Behold, the Lamb of God!" The two disciples heard him say this, and they followed Jesus. Jesus turned and saw them following and said to them, "What are you seeking?" And they said to him, "Rabbi" (which means Teacher), "where are you staying?" He said to them, "Come and you will see." So they came and saw where he was staying, and they stayed with him that day, for it was about the tenth hour.

JOHN 1:35–39 ESV

3. Why do you think John's two disciples followed Jesus? Knowing the answer to His question already, why do think Jesus asked them, "What are you seeking?"

4. Jesus is with you always, and your sins are forgiven because of His sacrifice on the cross and His victory over sin and death. Knowing this truth, how would you answer His question, "What are you seeking?" Or, considered another way, "What are you waiting on?"

Take a moment to reflect on everything you have experienced on your Advent journey. Jesus arrived amidst the sheep of Bethlehem as they were being raised to serve as sacrifices at Jerusalem's temple. Thirty-three years later, and just six miles from where He was born, Jesus would be the last of Bethlehem's sheep. Crucified for your sins, dead and buried, Christ would come back to life three days later. Though we are still longing to experience everything God has promised, and we wait for our ultimate redemption—one wait is already over. Christ has come. Our sins are forgiven. Death has been defeated. Love has won!

5. Looking back on your Advent experience during this study, how would you describe your relationship with God? What has changed over the past four weeks?

Connect & Discuss

The last few days before Christmas are often packed with parties, gatherings, shared meals, gift exchanges, and last-minute shopping. But in the flurry of activity before the big day, it's easy to lose sight of the baby in the manger waiting there for you. So take some time today to reach out to someone and describe your experience during this season of Advent before spending a few minutes sharing your requests and praying together. If you're part of a group completing this study, connect with a fellow group member and discuss some of your insights from your final session. Use any of the following prompts to help you connect and wait on God together.

What have you enjoyed most about this Christmas season? Why?

How has observing Advent as a season of expectant waiting enhanced your holiday season?

What is one of the ways God has revealed He is waiting for you during the course of this study?

What have you discovered about God by waiting on Him and with Him these past four weeks?

How has this study influenced how you will prepare for Christmas next year?

How will you pray for one another as you prepare to celebrate Christmas?

Worship While You Wait

You may already have plans to attend a church gathering on Christmas Eve or Christmas Day. Perhaps you have family celebrating at your home, or you might be traveling to see loved ones. And, of course, there's actually celebrating Christmas Day, complete with all the plans you've been making for the past weeks or even months. This is all the more reason to use this final Advent worship time as a way of enjoying solitude and reflection to draw closer to God.

While it may be more challenging than prior weeks, set aside fifteen minutes and find a spot where you won't be interrupted or distracted. Light all four candles on your Advent wreath and dim the other lights nearby. Think back to the first week when you began this study and first paused to worship while you wait. What has changed that you didn't expect? What's been different about this holiday season compared to others? How are you experiencing God's presence right now? Use the following questions and prompts to aid in your reflection.

> Amidst the busyness of the next couple days, take a few minutes to close your eyes and still your heart before the Lord. Clear out the jumble of thoughts about all you still need to do and all that you're about to experience as you celebrate Christmas.

> What do you need most from God right now in order to enjoy Christmas Day? Are you craving peace and quiet in the midst of guests visiting and routines being suspended—or are you feeling lonely and left out because you're mostly on your own this year? Whatever you are experiencing, open your heart and invite God's Spirit to embrace you with peace.

Looking back over the past four weeks, what are you most thankful for? Why?

What do you sense God communicating to you consistently during this season of Advent? What next steps does He want you to take?

What God ordains is always good:

His will is just and holy.

As He directs my life for me,

I follow meek and lowly.

My God indeed

In ev'ry need

Knows well how He will shield me;

To Him, then, I will yield me.

What God ordains is always good:

He never will deceive me;

He leads me in His righteous way,

And never will He leave me.

I take content

What He has sent;

His hand that sends me sadness

Will turn my tears to gladness.

"WHAT'ER MY GOD ORDAINS IS RIGHT"
SAMUEL RODIGAST (1649–1708)

Leader's Guide

Thank you for your willingness to lead your group through this study! What you have chosen to do is valuable and will make a positive difference in the lives of others. The rewards of being a leader are different from those of participating, and we hope that as you lead you will find your own journey with Jesus deepened by this experience.

Waiting Here for You is a four-session Bible study built around video content and small-group interaction. As the group leader, imagine yourself as the host of a party. Your job is to take care of your guests by managing the details so that when your guests arrive, they can focus on one another and on the interaction around the topic for that session.

Your role as the group leader is not to answer all the questions or reteach the content—the video, book, and study guide will do most of that work. Your job is to guide the experience and cultivate your small group into a connected and engaged community. This will make it a place for members to process, question, and reflect—not necessarily receive more instruction.

There are several elements in this leader's guide that will help you as you structure your study and reflection time, so be sure to follow along and take advantage of each one.

Before You Begin

Before your first meeting, make sure the group members have a copy of this study guide. Alternately, you can hand out the study guides at your first meeting and give each person some time to look over the material and ask any preliminary questions. Make sure they are aware that they have access to the streaming videos at any time by following the instructions provided. During your first time together, ask the members to provide their name and contact information so you can keep in touch with them.

Generally, the ideal size for a group is eight to ten people, which will ensure that everyone has enough time to participate in discussions. If you have more people, you might want to break up the main group into smaller subgroups. Encourage those who show up at the first meeting to commit to attending the duration of the study, as this will help the group members get to know one another, create stability for the group, and help you know how to best prepare to lead them through the material.

Each of the sessions begins with an opening reflection in the Welcome section. The questions that follow in the Connect section serve as an icebreaker to get the group members thinking about the topic. Some people may want to tell a long story in response to one of these questions, but the goal is to keep the answers brief. Ideally, you want everyone in the group to get a chance to answer, so try to keep the responses to a minute or less. If you have talkative group members, say up front that everyone needs to keep their answers brief.

Give the group members a chance to answer, but also tell them to feel free to pass if they wish. With the rest of the study, it's generally not a good idea to have everyone answer every question—a free-flowing discussion is more desirable. But with the opening icebreaker questions, you can go around the circle. Encourage shy people to share, but don't force them.

At your first meeting, let the members know each session contains a personal study section they can use to continue to engage with the content until the next meeting. While this is optional, it will help them cement the concepts presented during the group study time. Let them know that if they choose to do so, they can watch the video for the next session by accessing the streaming code provided. Invite them to bring any questions and insights to your next meeting, especially if they had a breakthrough moment or didn't understand something.

Preparation for Each Session

As the leader, there are a few things you should do to prepare for each meeting:

- **Read through the session.** This will help you become more familiar with the content and know how to structure the discussion times.

- **Decide how the videos will be used.** Determine whether you want the members to watch the videos ahead of time (again, via the streaming access code found on the inside front cover) or together as a group.

- **Decide which questions you want to discuss.** Based on the length of your group discussions, you may not be able to get through all the questions. So look over the questions and choose which ones you definitely want to cover.

- **Be familiar with the questions you want to discuss.** When the group meets, you'll be watching the clock, so make sure you are familiar with the questions you have selected. In this way, you will ensure that you have the material at the forefront of your mind.

- **Pray for your group.** Pray for your group members and ask God to lead them as they study His Word.

In many cases, there will be no one "right" answer to the question. Answers will vary, especially when the members are being asked to share their personal experiences.

Structuring the Discussion Time

You will need to determine how long you want to meet so you can plan your time accordingly. Suggested times for each section have been provided in this study guide, and if you adhere to these times, your group will meet for ninety minutes. If you want to meet for two hours, follow the times given in the right-hand column:

Section	90 Minutes	120 Minutes
CONNECT (discuss one or more of the opening questions for the session)	15 minutes	20 minutes
WATCH (watch the teaching material together and take notes)	20 minutes	20 minutes
DISCUSS (discuss the study questions you selected ahead of time)	35 minutes	50 minutes
RESPOND (write down key takeaways)	10 minutes	15 minutes
PRAY (pray together and dismiss)	10 minutes	15 minutes

It is up to you to keep things on schedule. You might want to set a timer for each segment so both you and the group members know when your time is up. (There are some good phone apps for timers that play a gentle chime or other upbeat sounds instead of a disruptive noise.)

Don't be concerned if the group members are quiet or slow to share. People are often quiet when they are pulling together their ideas, and this might be a new experience for them. Just ask a question and let it hang in the air until someone shares. You can then say, "Thank you. What about others? What came to you when you watched that portion of the teaching?"

Group Dynamics

Leading a group through *Waiting Here for You* will be rewarding both to you and your group. But you still may encounter challenges along the way! Discussions can get off track. Group members may not be sensitive to the needs and ideas of others. Some might worry they will be expected to talk about matters that make them feel awkward. Others may express comments that result in disagreements. To help ease this strain on you and the group, consider the following ground rules:

- When someone raises a question or comment that is off the main topic, suggest that you deal with it another time, or, if you feel led to go in that direction, let the group know you will be spending some time discussing it.

- If someone asks a question that you don't know how to answer, admit it and move on. At your discretion, feel free to invite group members to comment on questions that call for personal experience.

- If you find that one or two people are dominating the discussion time, direct a few questions to others in the group. Outside the main group time, ask the more dominating members to help you draw out the quieter ones. Work to make them a part of the solution instead of part of the problem.

- When a disagreement occurs, encourage the members to process the matter in love. Encourage those on opposite sides to restate what they heard the other side say about the matter, and then invite each side to evaluate if that is accurate. Lead the group in examining other scriptures related to the topic and look for common ground.

When any of these issues arise, encourage your group members to follow these words from Scripture: "Love one another" (John 13:34), "If it is possible, as far as it depends on you, live at peace with everyone" (Romans 12:18), "Whatever is true . . . noble . . . right . . . if anything is excellent or praiseworthy—think about such things" (Philippians 4:8), and "Be quick to listen, slow to speak and slow to become angry" (James 1:19).

Thank you again for taking the time to lead your group. You are making a difference in your group members' lives and having an impact on their journey as they learn what it means to wait on God and with God during this Advent season.

About the Author

Louie Giglio is pastor of Passion City Church and the original visionary of the Passion movement, which exists to call a generation to leverage their lives for the fame of Jesus. Since 1997, Passion Conferences have gathered college-aged young people in events across the United States and around the world.

Louie is the national-bestselling author of over a dozen books, including *Seeing God as a Perfect Father, Don't Give the Enemy a Seat at Your Table, At the Table with Jesus, Goliath Must Fall, Indescribable: 100 Devotions About God and Science, The Comeback, The Air I Breathe, I Am Not but I Know I Am,* and others. As a communicator, he is widely known for messages such as "Indescribable" and "How Great Is Our God."

An Atlanta native and graduate of Georgia State University, Louie has done postgraduate work at Baylor University and holds a master's degree from Southwestern Baptist Theological Seminary. Louie and his wife, Shelley, make their home in Atlanta.

Video Study for Your
Church or Small Group

In this six-session video Bible study, bestselling author and pastor Louie Giglio helps you apply the principles in *Don't Give the Enemy a Seat at Your Table* to your life. The study guide includes access to six streaming video sessions, video notes and a comprehensive structure for group discussion time, and personal study for deeper reflection between sessions.

Study Guide + Streaming Video
9780310156284

DVD
9780310134268

Available now at your favorite bookstore
or streaming video on StudyGateway.com.

 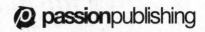